OFFICIAL ANNUAL
1997

Written by
Douglas G. Russell

Edited by John C. Traynor

C O N T E N T S

SCOTTISH C
ERS 1996

C O N T E N T S

SIMPLY GAZZA

Premier League, 28th April 1996

RANGERS 3   **ABERDEEN 1**

Gascoigne (21, 81 and 86 mins)

THE FACT of the matter was that if Rangers were to defeat Aberdeen at Ibrox in the second-last game of the season, they would retain the Championship and 'eight-in-a-row' would become reality. Close rivals Celtic were one point behind, having played one game more than the 'Light Blues'. It was all down to Rangers.

Of course, Aberdeen were intent on spoiling any possible Rangers party and after Brian Irvine's goal in nineteen minutes, it seemed momentarily as if the men from the north may cause an upset. 'Momentarily' was the key word, as within two minutes, Rangers equalised.

A Laudrup corner to Gascoigne on the edge of the box. The midfielder swept past Dodds, brushed aside Windass and curled a soaring right-foot shot over goalkeeper Watt. An absolute cracker! After that, Rangers dominated but failed to take the lead. Alan McLaren twice struck woodwork from headed attempts.

With barely ten minutes of the game remaining, it seemed to be heading for a draw. It was time for 'Scotland's Player of the Year' to step forward and become immortal.

'Gazza' gathered the ball in his own half and set off on a run, holding off challenge after Aberdeen challenge before steering a left-foot shot past Watt to score one of the finest individual goals ever witnessed at Ibrox.

His 'hat-trick' was completed from the penalty spot five minutes later after Gordon Durie had been brought down in full flight. All credit to Ally for allowing 'Gazza' to take it!

All Championships are naturally special occasions and this was number 46. As the club's adopted anthem echoed throughout the stadium, the fans celebrated another triumphant year. Rangers had once again proved themselves 'Simply the Best' – but for today, it was 'Simply Gazza'.

GOAL No. 1

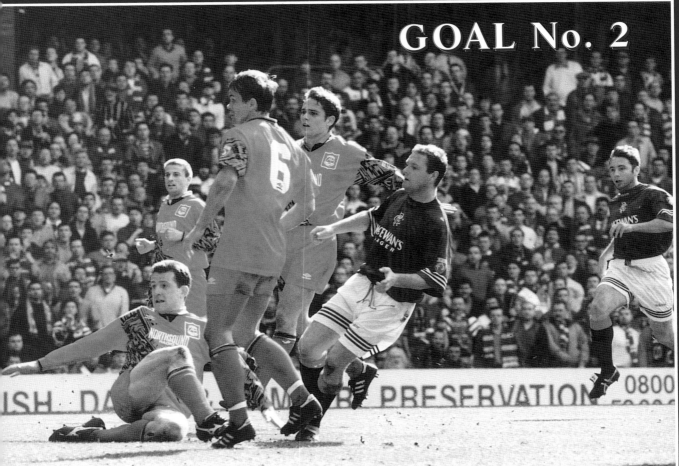

GOAL No. 2

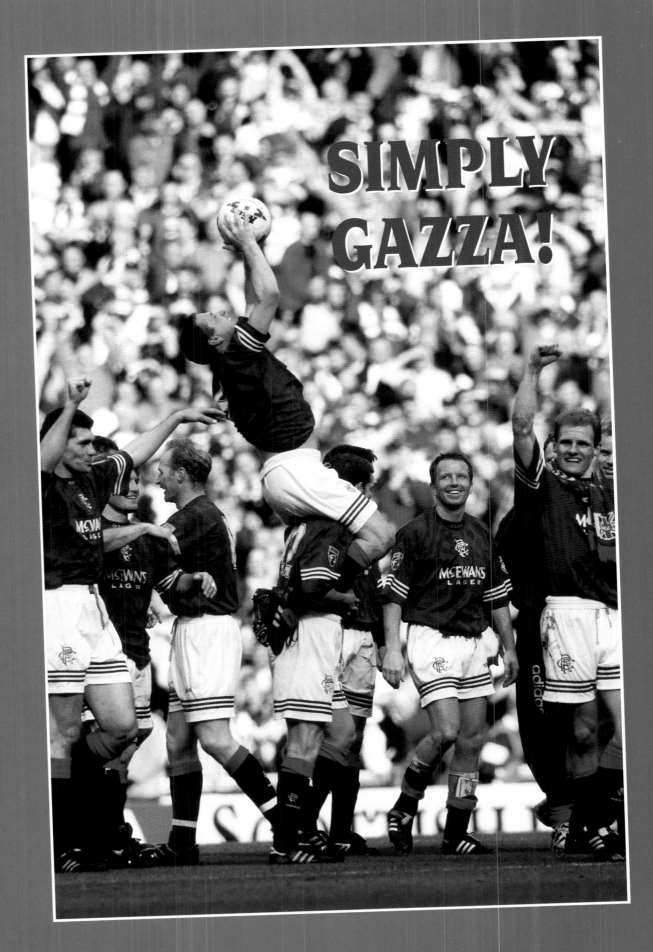

SIMPLY GAZZA!

SIMPLY GAZZA!

A MAN FOR ALL SEASONS

Richard Gough

AFTER RANGERS had clinched their eighth successive Championship, manager Walter Smith suggested that, had it not been for injury, inspirational club captain Richard Gough could well have been voted 'Player of the Year' 1995/96

Certainly his form that season was quite awe-inspiring as the 'Light Blues' faced up to the challenge of a born-again Celtic from across the city. Many were even calling for his return to the international squad as it was difficult to comprehend how a defender of his calibre could be missing from the dark blue of Scotland.

Significantly, the first match Richard missed through injury was the Coca-Cola League Cup Semi-Final against Aberdeen at Hampden. Rangers lost 2-1. After that he was an ever-present in the starting line-up until early February, when John Brown took his place at Firhill prior to Rangers' 2-1 victory.

Surprisingly, the captain, was top scorer in that disappointing 'Champions League' series of games. He netted twice against, firstly, Borussia Dortmund at Ibrox and then away to Italian Champions Juventus.

As the season entered its final phase with the possibility still remaining of either side of the 'Old Firm' taking the Championship, Richard returned to take his rightful place at the heart of that Rangers defence for the last few crucial games.

Bandaged after a nasty head clash with Brian Irvine at the start of the Championship decider against Aberdeen at Ibrox, Richard commandingly led his team to another memorable victory. There was no one prouder as he held aloft the League Championship trophy that sunny April day. He had been there way back in Season 1988/89 when it all began.

Not just a man for eight seasons – A MAN FOR ALL SEASONS.

. . . . . there's only ONE

PAUL GASCOIGNE!

The Never-Ending Story

Ally McCoist M.B.E.

PICTURE the scene: Kirkcaldy, late March 1996, nearing the climax of the '95/'96 Championship race.

Rangers are not playing well and with barely seven minutes remaining, are losing 2-1 to Raith Rovers. It would seem that the Ibrox men are heading for their first "away" defeat of that long hard season.

Enter 'The Magician' to conjure up victory when all seemed lost!

Following a Gascoigne corner and Petric's subsequent header across the face of the goal, Ally equalised with a powerful header. The 'McCoist Show' was now well and truly on the road as, moments later, another headed attempt flashed just past the post. Then Geddes pulled off a quite magnificent save from a blistering shot on the run as Ally pushed for his 'hat-trick'.

Mr M.B.E. was not to be denied, however, and after another Paul Gascoigne corner, the veteran striker 'won' the match for Rangers. The relief both on and off the park was there for all to see. Gordon Durie added icing to the cake scoring No. 4 right at the end from the penalty spot.

It would be virtually impossible to detail the number of so-called 'important' goals that McCoist has scored in his astonishing career with Rangers. Just as another compilation of his exploits is finalised, additional pages are required to update this seemingly never-ending story.

Few would dispute that, at the ripe old age of 33, he remains the best goalscorer around, with still more to come. For once the word 'legend' is no exaggeration.

Ally in action against Hibernian (Top) and Borussia Dortmund in the '95/'96 Champions League. Both games at Ibrox.

Rangers Rampage

Premier League, 30th December 1995

RANGERS 7   HIBERNIAN 0

Miller (30 mins)
Durie (40, 52, 77 and 86 mins)
Gascoigne (76 mins)
Salenko (83 mins)

IT WAS a confident Hibernian team that travelled west to Ibrox in December 1995 on the trail of Premier League points. Currently sitting third in the Championship table, the Edinburgh outfit were the only side to have inflicted defeat on Rangers (home or away) in that campaign.

Both sets of supporters anticipated a memorable match on an extremely cold winter's afternoon. In retrospect, 'memorable' proved to be something of an understatement as far as the Rangers fans were concerned. The Champions ran riot, giving the 'Follow Follow' legions the best possible reason for beginning the New Year celebrations a day early.

GOAL No. 1

The sequence of events as the 'Light Blues' recorded their biggest League victory since 1987 (when Morton suffered a similar seven-goal thrashing) was as follows:

No 1 – Charlie Miller stroked home following a Gordon Durie through-ball.

No 2 – A diving Durie header after delightful wing-play and cross courtesy of Brian Laudrup.

No 3 – 'Jukie' again, superbly chipping Jim Leighton from 18 yards.

No 4 – The 'goal of the game' as Gazza displayed outstanding skills dancing past numerous Hibs defenders to score.

No 5 – Durie's 'hat-trick', slipping the ball past Leighton after a Laudrup pass.

No 6 – Oleg Salenko bustled through the Hibs defence to score his eighth of the season.

No 7 – That man Durie again, driving home from a crowded penalty area.

A dazzling display by Rangers, easily their best of the season so far.

As for Gazza's goal, quite simply one of those special Christmas treats that linger long in the memory.

ROBBO'S RETURN

David Robertson

NO DOUBT memories of his previous Scottish Cup semi-final appearance against Celtic were in the mind of the Rangers full-back when David Robertson returned to duty on 7th April 1996 (after having missed the previous three games through suspension and injury) in a re-run of that now famous confrontation.

March 31st, 1992 is already part of Ibrox folklore, the date of an understandably famous 10-man victory over Celtic in the year that Rangers achieved their first Scottish Cup triumph in eleven years. 'Robbo', of course, was the 'missing' man that night, having been dismissed only six minutes into the game for a bodycheck on Joe Miller – without even touching the ball!

Some four years on and Scotland's 'Big Two' would meet again head-to-head in the quest for cup glory. David's contribution in a notable 2-1 victory over the holders included an assist in Rangers' opening goal, when a right-foot shot could only be parried by 'keeper Marshall for predator Ally McCoist to convert.

Another Hampden date in May now awaited the player who many have forgotten has actually scored in the final of this competition. That was against Celtic when Aberdeen lifted the trophy in 1990 after an epic penalty shoot-out which ended 9-8 in their favour.

However, few Rangers fans will have forgotten his so-called 'off-side' goal against Celtic in the 3-3 draw at Ibrox, November 1995. Although celebrations were cut short that day, April's cup result more then compensated.

Unlike a certain evening back in 1992, on this occasion the defender had played a major role in his team's progress to the final.

'ROBBO'S RETURN', INDEED.

THE HUNGER

Scottish Cup Semi-Final, 7th April 1996

CELTIC 1

RANGERS 2
McCoist (43 mins)
Laudrup (67 mins)

THE TIME had come. Questions would be answered. Both teams entered the fray in remarkably high spirits after their previous outings a week earlier on Premier League duty. Rangers had snatched victory from the jaws of defeat against Raith Rovers at Kirkcaldy, eventually winning 4-2, whilst Celtic had completed a 5-0 demolition job on Aberdeen at Parkhead.

Although an even game seemed in prospect, the truth of the matter was that the Ibrox men controlled events for eighty minutes until Celtic scored near the end, to produce a nerve-jangling finish. After 'Super' Ally had missed a good scoring opportunity in seventeen minutes, the striker made amends just before the break to give his side the lead after fine work by David Robertson.

Rangers' second in sixty-seven minutes was an absolute gem of one-touch football. Gascoigne to Laudrup, Laudrup to Durie on the right and then Durie back inside for the 'Prince of Players', controlling the high ball on his chest, to move away from the Celtic rearguard. His subsequent lob from outside the penalty area over the advancing Marshall completed a majestic, flowing movement.

Rangers had proved once again that theirs was the greater hunger for glory as they despatched the holders and headed for a final confrontation with Hearts on May 18th.!

That would be another story but one thing was certain – the 'Follow, Follow' boys could relax in the knowledge that they had already witnessed one of the goals of the season courtesy of the 'Great Dane'.

YES, IT WAS AS GOOD AS THAT.

Laudrup's stunning second goal.

BRAVEHEART

Stuart McCall

FEW WOULD dispute that he is, indeed, one of the genuine *competitors* in Scottish football.

Cast your mind back to Stuart's tigerish 'Man of the Match' display in the Scottish Cup semi-final against Celtic in April 1996 (when he deputised for the injured Richard Gough as Rangers' captain) if any further proof is required. He seemed to cover every blade of Hampden grass that day, driving Rangers on to another memorable victory.

Naturally there are other aspects to his game, including the occasional, but important, goal. It was Stuart's strike against Kilmarnock with barely 10 minutes remaining in the first game of Season 1995/96 that ensured full points at the start of another long campaign. Certainly just as important was his goal (Rangers' first) in the difficult late-season away match at Fir Park, Motherwell. The 3-1 triumph ensured that the Champions remained on course for 'Eight-In-A-Row' with only two games remaining.

Summer 1996 – and Stuart headed south of the border as a member of the Scotland pool for the European Championship finals in England. It was in Season 1991/92 that the player travelled in the opposite direction from Merseyside to join Rangers on transfer from Everton. Since then he has become an indispensable part of Rangers' midfield.

Maybe he would not have been an obvious choice to play Scottish freedom fighter William Wallace in Mel Gibson's Oscar-winning film. Even though the accent is not quite right, a true 'Braveheart' nevertheless.

> **Opposite, Top:** *Stuart in typically combative midfield action versus Aberdeen at Pittodrie.*
> **Bottom:** *The vital late strike in the opening game of Season 1995/96 versus Kilmarnock at Ibrox.*

RANGERS 4 CELTIC 0

Top Left: *Ally McCoist powers home Rangers' second goal with his head, 3-3 at Ibrox, November 1995.*
Bottom Left: *Another 'Super' header for the only goal of the 1-0 Coca Cola Cup victory, Parkhead, September 1995.*
Top Right: *Brian Laudrup's opening goal in the 3-3 thriller at Ibrox, November 1995.*
Bottom Right: *Alan McLaren gives Rangers the lead at Ibrox, Mothers' Day, March 1996 in 1-1 draw.*

LORD OF THE DANCE

Scottish Cup Final, 18th May 1996
RANGERS   5   HEARTS   1
Laudrup (37 and 49 mins)
Durie (66, 79 and 85 mins)

IF THE PENULTIMATE League game against Aberdeen at Ibrox in Season 1995/96 was all Gazza's glory, the Scottish Cup Final belonged to another Rangers genius. His performance that afternoon was such that in years to come, the 1996 final will simply be remembered as the day of Brian Laudrup.

A close game had been anticipated with many pundits even forecasting a Hearts victory. Few would have reckoned with the total destruction of the Tynecastle club that was to follow, however.

The champions' opening goal in thirty-seven minutes saw Durie and Laudrup combine in midfield before the Scot lofted a delightful ball beyond the Hearts defence for the advancing Dane to finish with deadly accuracy. Rangers could well have increased their lead in the first half courtesy of either Gough, Gascoigne or Durie but the advantage remained at just one goal when the whistle sounded.

Although the 'Light Blues' second goal followed a blunder by Gilles Rousset when a Laudrup cross slipped through his legs, goals three, four and five were all fine creations. Gordon Durie's first in sixty-six minutes was a stunning right-foot volley on the run following Laudrup's cross to complete a fine flowing movement between the pair.

Colquhoun pulled one back for Hearts but their fate had already been sealed. Goals four and five were both created by Brian Laudrup and converted by Gordon Durie. In seventy-nine minutes the striker completed his 'double' from close in and six minutes later, headed home to complete his 'hat-trick' and a quite emphatic victory.

Of course Gordon Durie deserved much praise for his goalscoring achievement that day. After all, it was the first 'hat-trick' in a Scottish Cup Final since 1972 and only the third in its entire history. But Laudrup's performance . . . that was something else again.

In footballing terms, only a select band are touched by genius. Step forward the maestro, Brian Laudrup.

Brian Laudrup's deadly finish for Goal No. 1 and (Below) Gordon Durie's stunning volley on the run for No. 3

MEMORIES OF

SEASON 1988/89 . . . SEASON 1988/89 . . . SEASON 1988/89 . . . SEASON

Highlights included 5-1 and 4-1 demolitions of Celtic. Championship secured at Ibrox on April 29th with 4-0 victory over Hearts. The season of Ian Durrant's horrific injury at Aberdeen.

SEASON 1990/91 . . . SEASON 1990/91 . . . SEASO

Mark Hateley joined from Monaco. Manager Gr[...] join Liverpool (with just four games remaining) a[...] promoted. Exciting season climaxed at Ibrox on [...] 'winner-take-all' game against Aberdeen which r[...] 2-0 victory, Hateley scoring both goals.

SEASON 1991/92 . . . SEASON 1991/92 . . . SEASON 1991/92 . . . SEASON

The year of Ally McCoist, as he became the first Scot to win Europe's 'Golden Boot'. His partnership with Mark Hateley was deadly. Champions again on April 18th at Ibrox through 4-0 victory over St Mirren.

SEASON 1993/94 . . . SEASON 1993/94 . . . SEASON 1993/94 . . . SEASON

Mark Hateley became the first Englishman to be voted Scotland's 'Player of the Year' by the Football Writers' Association. Celtic were blown away at Parkhead on January 1st as Rangers stormed 3-0 up in the first half-hour. Championship secured by a 22-match unbeaten run between December and April.

SEASON 1995/96 . . . SEASON 19

Quite simply, it belonged to on[...]

'EIGHT-IN-A-ROW'

SEASON 1989/90 . . . SEASON 1989/90 . . . SEASON 1989/90 . . . SEASON

The arrival of former Celtic player Maurice Johnston from Nantes made all the headlines – as did his last-minute winner against his ex-colleagues at Ibrox on November 4th. Trevor Steven's goal in the 1-0 victory over Dundee United at Tannadice in April retained the Premier title.

91 . . . SEASON

ouness left to
er Smith was
th with
n that famous

SEASON 1992/93 . . . SEASON 1992/93 . . . SEASON 1992/93 . . . SEASON

One of the great years in Rangers history. Victory over English Champions, Leeds United, in the 'Battle of Britain' and an unbeaten run in the 'Champions League' against Marseille, Bruges and CSKA Moscow. Gary McSwegan scored the only goal of the game against Airdrie at Broomfield and it was 'FIVE-IN-A-ROW'.

SEASON 1994/95 . . . SEASON 1994/95 . . . SEASON 1994/95 . . . SEASON

Brian Laudrup's season, without a doubt! The 'Great Dane' was hugely influential as consecutive title No. 7 was secured by a comfortable fifteen points from Motherwell. Brian's strike against Celtic in the 3-1 Hampden victory in October was, for many, the goal of the season.

. . SEASON 1995/96 . . . SEASON

. . . . Paul Gascoigne!

MAC THE KNIFE

Alan McLaren

SOME WOULD suggest that Season 1995/96 was the time when Alan McLaren actually 'came of age' as a Rangers player.

His first outing in Rangers colours had been the memorable 3-1 victory over Celtic at Hampden on Premier League duty back in October 1994. In the absence of the usual steadying influence of Richard Gough through injury, Alan's contribution to the Ibrox cause that day was quite immense.

With the arrival of Gordan Petric from Dundee United, Rangers began to operate with three central defenders. The more traditional 'Flat Back Four' system would be employed only occasionally dependent upon circumstances at the time.

Within this formation, Alan proved to be one of the 'Light Blues' most consistent players of the season, constantly earning praise on a weekly basis.

The so-called 'crunch' match against Celtic in the Premier League at Ibrox in March had been eagerly anticipated by most of Scottish Football. 'Mac' chose this occasion to score his first goal as a Rangers player against the other half of the 'Old Firm' in the 1-1 draw. This was a game that the Champions should really have won. (Even after Hughes' headed equaliser with only three minutes remaining, Rangers could have scored twice!)

Alan McLaren was deservedly awarded the 'Man of the Match' prize after the game. It wouldn't take 'Mystic Meg' from the B.B.C.'s weekly National Lottery show to predict more of those for this accomplished young player.

ACTION

Ian Ferguson

PORTRAITS

Alan McLaren

Stephen Wright

Alex
Cleland

ELECTRIC BLUE

CELTIC 0

RANGERS 2
Cleland (43 mins)
Gascoigne (56 mins)

HE CAME, he saw, he conquered. This had been the day, and indeed week, of Paul Gascoigne. Yet in many ways Celtic's confidence was understandable approaching this first 'Old Firm' league encounter (or maybe collision!) of the season. Rangers' greatest rivals were top of the table (one point ahead of the Light Blues) and had scored eight goals without loss in their previous two games, both 4-0 victories over Hearts and Dynamo Batumi in the European Cup Winners' Cup. Also, maybe just as significantly, Scotland's 'Player of the Year', Brian Laudrup, was missing from the Rangers ranks through injury. Gazza, however, was waiting to take centre stage. Let the show begin . . .

Though Celtic had the bulk of territorial advantage in the first half, the better chances were created by Rangers. Half-time stalemate was nearing when the visitors struck following good close control by Salenko on the right. His subsequent cross into the box resulted in a rare headed goal by Alex Cleland to give Rangers the lead at the interval.

The second period saw Gough's men become more and more dominant and it came as no great surprise when the lead was increased. And what a goal!

When Alan McLaren cleared from his own penalty area, Paul Gascoigne was positioned on the edge of the box close by. By the time Ally McCoist was sending a delightful ball into the Celtic area, Gazza was there to finish the move and guide the ball past the wrong-footed Marshall after a surging, strength-sapping sixty-yard run. Not bad for a so-called overweight player – and how he enjoyed celebrating with the Rangers support!

The Champions finished the game in style with Cleland almost adding a third near the end. This had been a super team performance with Captain Richard Gough quite immense at the heart of that solid defence, ably supported by McLaren and Petric.

Understandably, however, Gazza was the main topic of conversation. No-one would begrudge him the accolades this day at the end of a week in which the player had also turned in a superlative show against the Champions of Germany, Borussia Dortmund, at Ibrox the previous Wednesday evening. This was just the beginning, as much more magic would be seen in the weeks and months to come. But for now this convincing victory at Parkhead was more than enough.

In the world of advertising both 'Scottish Gas' and 'Scottish Power' loudly proclaim the virtues of their opposing kitchen fuels. Somehow, this day, the Champions had managed to combine both.

A new 'power' slogan for Scotland: "Electric Rangers - Cooking with 'Gas'!"

SWING LOW SWEET CHARIOT

Paul Gascoigne

THE SCEPTICS suggested that Rangers were making a huge mistake by spending £4.3 million to sign Paul Gascoigne in the summer of 1995. After all they said, he had only played a total of 47 games in three seasons with Italian 'Serie A' club Lazio and was injury prone.

Less than twelve months later by the end of April 1996, 'Gazza' had competed in 41 matches, scored 19 goals and been voted 'Scotland's Player of the Year' by both his fellow professionals and the Scottish Football Writers' Association. His was the bright light that illuminated much of Scottish football.

As the season progressed, Paul just got better and better and finally

reached a peak of perfection against Aberdeen on that now famous late April Sunday. Along the way, of course, there were sublime moments to treasure – his stunning goal against Celtic in November after running the length of the park, Rangers' fourth in the 7-0 rout of Hibernian when he literally danced past numerous defenders to score, his 'Champions League' strike against Steaua Bucharest as the defenders of the East European team watched in wonder . . . the list goes on.

Paul's first award in Scotland as 'Player of the Month' in February 1996 was nicely complemented with a match-winning penalty kick in the 1-0 Pittodrie victory that same month. Aberdeen and awards would feature again in the not-too-distant future when, appropriately, 'Gazza' was destined to take centre stage, conjure up a performance of rare magic and thus cast a hypnotic spell over 47,000 people.

A footballer with true genius in his feet. Those sweet chariots were swinging low.

SEARCH FOR A HERO

John Brown

SOMETIMES IT is an unlikely hero who emerges from the sidelines to take centre stage at a crucial period of any Championship. Take the case of John Brown. The player with a Rangers heart started the season in his capacity as Reserve Coach with the possibility of regular first-team action seemingly rather remote.

Although he had taken his place in Rangers' starting line-up on one occasion (against Juventus at Ibrox in the Champions League, November 1995) prior to the turn of the year, this was due to Alan McLaren's suspension for that game.

The New Year brought a new set of circumstances. Rangers faced the prospect of two extremely tough away games in succession – Aberdeen at Pittodrie (February 25th) and then Hibernian at Easter Road (March 3rd). Club captain Richard Gough was still missing through injury for the trip to the 'Granite City'.

Enter 'Bomber'. John played superbly that day at the heart of the Rangers defence. His contribution to a 1-0 victory was quite significant, even managing a goal-line clearance to deny the Dons an equaliser. The following week saw the return of Richard Gough but sadly he had to be substituted at half-time injured in an extremely physical and bruising encounter. Enter 'Bomber' 2. Again his performance was quite splendid beside McLaren and Petric at the back.

Perhaps the fans fondest memory of John that season would be after the Scottish Cup Semi-Final victory over Celtic in April. As they celebrated, the player ran over and threw his jersey to them. Back in Season 1992/93, after that emotional 'Champions League' match against CSKA Moscow, you may remember he did the same thing.

ONE OF A RARE BREED.

FUN QUIZ
Season 1995/96

1. Who scored Rangers' first and last goals of the league season?

2. Name the young Rangers player who is patron of the Scottish Schools F.A.

3. Which Premier Division team did Paul Gascoigne fail to score against?

4. Mark Hateley's last goal for Rangers was against which club?

5. Stephen Wright missed two-thirds of the season through injury. When did it happen?

6. Who was Rangers' top scorer against Celtic?

7. On how many occasions have Rangers won the Championship in their history?

8. Name the player who threw his jersey to the fans after the Scottish Cup Semi-Final victory over Celtic?

9. At Ibrox, more people watched Morton in the League Cup than Borussia Dortmund in the Champions League. True or False?

10. Gordan Petric scored once for Rangers – against which team?

11. Two players scored 'hat-tricks' against Keith in the Scottish Cup. Who were they?

12. Name the Ranger who has worn both tartan and pink suits, albeit on different occasions.

Answers on page 54

CELEBRATIONS IN BLUE

Top: *Ally takes a bow after scoring the winner in the 3-2 victory over Motherwell at Ibrox, February 1996.*
Bottom: *Craig Moore celebrates his winning goal against Aberdeen at Pittodrie in the 1-0 victory, October 1995.*

Top: *Alan McLaren's jig of delight after opening the scoring versus Celtic, March 1996.* Bottom: *Erik Bo Andersen celebrates his two goals versus Falkirk, March 1996.*

DANISH BLUE 2

Erik Bo Andersen

AS TRANSFERS go, it had been a fairly low-key affair. Even after his first appearance in Rangers colours against Hibernian at Easter Road in March 1996, the jury, as the saying goes, was still out. The fans seemed to have reserved judgement.

Before the end of the following month, however, hero No. 2 from Denmark was being acclaimed as Erik Bo Andersen netted five times in his first two home Premier League games against Falkirk and Partick Thistle.

A 'hat-trick' is a considerable achievement for any new arrival but Bo's three against Thistle at Ibrox were actually something special. Quite special.

Celebrating an Andersen goal against Falkirk.

His first, in eighteen minutes, following a through-ball from countryman Brian Laudrup, was a viciously struck left-foot shot leaving goalkeeper Nicky Walker well beaten. Three minutes later and goal No. 2. A long ball out of defence from Alan McLaren saw the striker hold off a challenge from Thistle full-back McKee before rounding the 'keeper to net from a tight angle. For someone who appears rather slight, he certainly had little problem fending-off the defender. The trio was completed in sixty-three minutes with a downward header following a cross from – who else? – Brian Laudrup.

One week later, his goal against Motherwell just before half-time to give Rangers a 2-0 advantage, virtually secured those three precious points. The Ibrox legions were now of one mind – Andersen had arrived!

GORDON'S ALIVE

Gordon Durie

IT SAYS a great deal about Gordon Durie that, despite a troublesome hernia problem and subsequent operation, the striker ended the season at Hampden on 18th May 1996 by scoring a hat-trick and thus becoming top scorer at Ibrox with twenty-three goals. Quite an achievement considering that Gordon had missed some twenty games through injury that year.

This rich vein of goalscoring form not only ensured his inclusion in the Scotland squad for the European Championship Finals in England, but naturally helped Rangers stay ahead of Celtic in the season's quest for honours. In particular, Gordon's league goals during those dark December and January days were most important.

His winner (and only goal of the game) against Partick Thistle at Ibrox in early December was followed by a total of five goals against Kilmarnock and Hibernian later that month. A new year and January saw one against Falkirk at Brockville and then a double against Raith Rovers at home.

The 1995/96 Championship ensured medal number three for Gordon since returning to Scotland in November 1993 in a £1.2 million transfer from Tottenham Hotspur. As he admits himself, he has been privileged to play alongside some of the best, including Lineker and Sheringham at White Hart Lane and McCoist and Hateley at Ibrox.

Gordon's journey to Rangers via Chelsea and Tottenham had taken time and he has come a long way in more ways than one since he was a member of the Hibs team beaten by Aberdeen in the 1985 Skol Cup Final.

Someone once said that travel broadens the mind. In Gordon's case, travel has resulted in three medals . . . and counting!

HELLO, HELLO, I'M BACK AGAIN!

Brian Laudrup

INJURY ENSURED that the first half of Season 1995/96 had been a most difficult time for Scotland's 'Player of the Year', Brian Laudrup. By November, prepared and ready,

the 'Norse God' was back. Rangers fans would once again revel in witnessing the return of that unique style and flair that is the hallmark of Laudrup's game.

Brian's 'comeback' match was the 3-3 draw against Celtic at Ibrox on November 19th. He scored Rangers' opener that day. It seemed somehow inevitable that the best would be saved for Celtic. Witness the Scottish Cup Semi-Final in April and the Dane's winning strike, judged by many to be the goal of the season.

Week in, week out, defences all over the country would be tormented. Just ask the Hearts rearguard after his dazzling 'May Day' display of defence destruction at Hampden that secured the Scottish Cup. For good measure, Brian and his brother Michael tormented Scotland in a friendly international in Copenhagen prior to the European Championship Finals of Summer 1996.

There can be little doubt that the arrival of Paul Gascoigne at Ibrox helped ease the pressure of expecta-

Celebrating the opening goal of the 1996 Scottish Cup Final.

tion on Brian Laudrup after his all-conquering performances the previous year in a Rangers jersey.

Laudrup's tantalising form in the Spring of 1996 augured well for another tilt at the Champions' League by Rangers later that year. Fully fit and in-form, he would be a revelation in any company.

Come to think of it, Paul Gascoigne <u>and</u> Brian Laudrup both fully fit in the same team for a whole season? Imagine that scenario – now there's a mouthwatering prospect!

From The Trophy Room

Height 320mm (12½")

KIEV SAMOVAR
1987

THE RUSSIAN champions who were our European Cup first round opponents in Season 1987/88 were reckoned by many to be the finest club side in the world. Indeed, they formed the backbone of the Soviet national team at that time.

Despite this strength, Rangers travelled to the Ukraine and restricted Dynamo Kiev to a 1-0 victory before a partisan crowd of 100,000 in the first leg.

The return at Ibrox was steeped in controversy before a ball was kicked. The Soviets were infuriated by a shrewd tactical manoeuvre by the then manager, Graeme Souness, designed to restrict their sweeping style – he reduced the width of the pitch by a few yards!

When the game got underway, the atmosphere was electric and the noise deafening – so much so that even globe-trotting Rangers like Souness and Trevor Francis had never known its like. Rangers won 2-0 on the night to record a famous 2-1 aggregate victory.

Dynamo star, Oleg Kuznetzov, played in both legs and clearly impressed Souness, as he went on to join Rangers some three years later.

The commemorative Russian samovar (tea-urn) pictured opposite is one of our most unique and treasured trophies.

September 16th: First Leg   Dynamo Kiev 1 Rangers 0
Rangers: Woods; Nicholl, Phillips; Roberts, Souness, Butcher; D. Ferguson, Cohen (Kirkwood), McCoist, Durrant, McGregor.

September 30th: Second Leg Rangers 2   Dynamo Kiev 0
                                                     Falco (23),
                                                     McCoist (49)
Rangers: Woods; Nicholl, Phillips; McGregor, Souness, Butcher; Francis (Fleck), Falco, McCoist, Durrant, Cohen (Kirkwood).

GORAM'S GOAL

Andy Goram

THE FOOTBALL **historians would note that in Season 1995/96 Rangers met Celtic on six occasions (in the Premier League, Coca-Cola League Cup and Scottish Cup) without defeat. Three victories and three draws were the results.**

To remain unbeaten against their greatest rivals all year owed a great debt to the remarkable dependability of Andy Goram in goal. Instead of listing save after save, let's recall just two of the many outstanding examples of his goalkeeping art.

In the traditional 'Ne'erday' (well actually January 3rd in 1996 due to television commitments) encounter, the game was evenly balanced at 0-0 when Celtic midfielder Phil O'Donnell struck a blistering left-foot shot on the run from just outside the box. Goram's fingertips pushed the ball onto the post and Richard Gough cleared. A truly marvellous save.

Goram's fabulous save from O'Donnell (No. 6) in the 0-0 draw at Parkhead, 3rd January 1996.

The previous November, the fans had witnessed a fabulous 3-3 draw at Ibrox. Certainly one of the main talking points that day was Andy's quite miraculous stop from a point-blank Van Hooijdonk volley with the Rangers defence posted missing. Even now it's still difficult to believe the quality of that save to deny the Dutchman.

It has previously been said of Andy that it would be possible to count on the the fingers of one hand the mistakes he would make in a season. Reviewing the 1995/96 period, even that ridiculously low figure is difficult to reach.

And 'Goram's Goal'? Simply to be the best. Many think he already is!

ANSWERS
FUN QUIZ

1. Stuart McCall against Kilmarnock at Ibrox and Gordon Durie against Kilmarnock at Rugby Park. **2.** Charlie Miller. **3.** Raith Rovers. **4.** Stirling Albion in the Coca-Cola Cup Third Round. **5.** Against Juventus at Ibrox, 1.11.95. **6.** Who else? . . . Ally McCoist, with three goals. **7.** 46 times (a world record). **8.** John Brown. **9.** True! Nearly 43,000 as opposed to 33,000. **10.** Raith Rovers in a 2-2 draw at Kirkcaldy. **11.** Alex Cleland and Ian Ferguson. **12.** Well, it wasn't Brian Laudrup!

ACKNOWLEDGEMENTS

Designed by Douglas Russell and John Traynor, with special assistance from Lisa Russell.

Typesetting and Origination by Inglis Allen, Kirkcaldy.

Bound in Scotland by Hunter & Foulis, Edinburgh.

All photographs supplied by *The Sun*

Picture Editor: Mark Sweeney

Photographers: Steve Welsh, Alan Ewing, Andy Barr, Peter Kelly, John Kirkby, Joe Campbell, Kenny Ramsay.

Every effort has been made by the publishers to ensure the accuracy of all details and information in this publication.

Printed and Published in Scotland by

INGLIS ALLEN

40 Townsend Place, Kirkcaldy, Fife, Scotland KY1 1HF.
Telephone (01592) 267201   Fax (01592) 206049
ISBN 1-8995990-0-2 © Inglis Allen 1996. All rights reserved.